British Library Cataloguing in Publication Data

A catalogue record for this book is
available from the British Library.

ISBN 0340 87865 7

First published in hardback in 2004

Published by Hodder Children's Books,
a division of Hodder Headline Limited,
338 Euston Road, London NW1 3BH

10 9 8 7 6 5 4 3 2 1

Printed in Hong Kong

BEACHMOLES AND BELLVINE

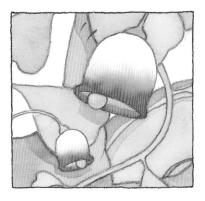

MICK INKPEN

Hodder
Children's
Books

A division of Hodder Headline Limited

The story starts like this. It is just after dawn on Blue Nose Island as Ploo's front door opens. Out rushes Dig. He is desperate to sniff out the beachmole that lives under Blue Nose Beach, though he has never yet come close to catching it.

Ploo follows.

'Come on, Dig!' he says. And straight away Dig stops his sniffing and runs to Ploo's side.

Why is Ploo up so early?

And where is he going?

He is off to the junglywood with an idea in his head.

In the junglywood Ploo listens for a sound,
 a particular sound. And almost immediately
there it is, the distant sound of tinkling bells.
This he follows until he comes to the foot of a
great, creeping vine, a bellvine.

Ploo's idea, you see, is to plant a bellvine
outside his house, so that its little bells will tinkle
in the breezes that blow across Blue Nose Beach.
And to do that he must grow a bellvine of his own.
And to do that he must collect some seeds.
And to do that he must climb the bellvine.
Or so he thinks.

But, as you can see, it is Dig who finds them,
just lying about on the ground.

Five little bellvine seeds.

At home, Ploo plants the seeds, each in its own little pot, and for three days he watches and waits. As it turns out only one of the seeds grows, but since one is all he needs, Ploo is not disappointed.

And how it grows! By the afternoon it has already made a tiny little bell, which tinkles as Ploo shakes the pot.

'Let's plant it out today!' says Ploo to Dig.

But Dig is not interested in the bellvine. He prefers to sniff up and down Blue Nose Beach looking for the beachmole, while Ploo plants the bellvine just outside his front door, with a little stick for it to lean on and plenty of water to drink.

By the evening Ploo is amazed to see that his bellvine has already grown taller than himself. And now it has three little bells which make a lovely sound every time he opens his front door.

Ding! Ding! Ding!

Ding! Ding! Ding! Ding! Ding!

It is the following morning and Ploo is waking to the sound of ringing, and something tickling his nose.

'Get off, Dig!' he says. But it is not Dig. It is the bellvine. It has grown right through his bedroom window!

'Oh dear!' says Ploo.

All day long Ploo snips off bits of the bellvine to keep it in check. But the more he snips, the more it seems to grow. And by the evening it has sent tendrily fingers all over his house. It has even stopped him getting through his own front door!

'You'd better sleep at my house tonight,' says his best friend, Hatz.

So that night Ploo and Dig go to sleep in Hatz' house. Or rather they don't, because in the night a strong wind blows up and Ploo cannot sleep for all the rustling of the bellvine leaves and all the ringing and the dinging of its bells. He tosses and turns and buries his head under the pillow.

And in the morning he looks out to find that the bellvine . . .

. . .has taken over everything!

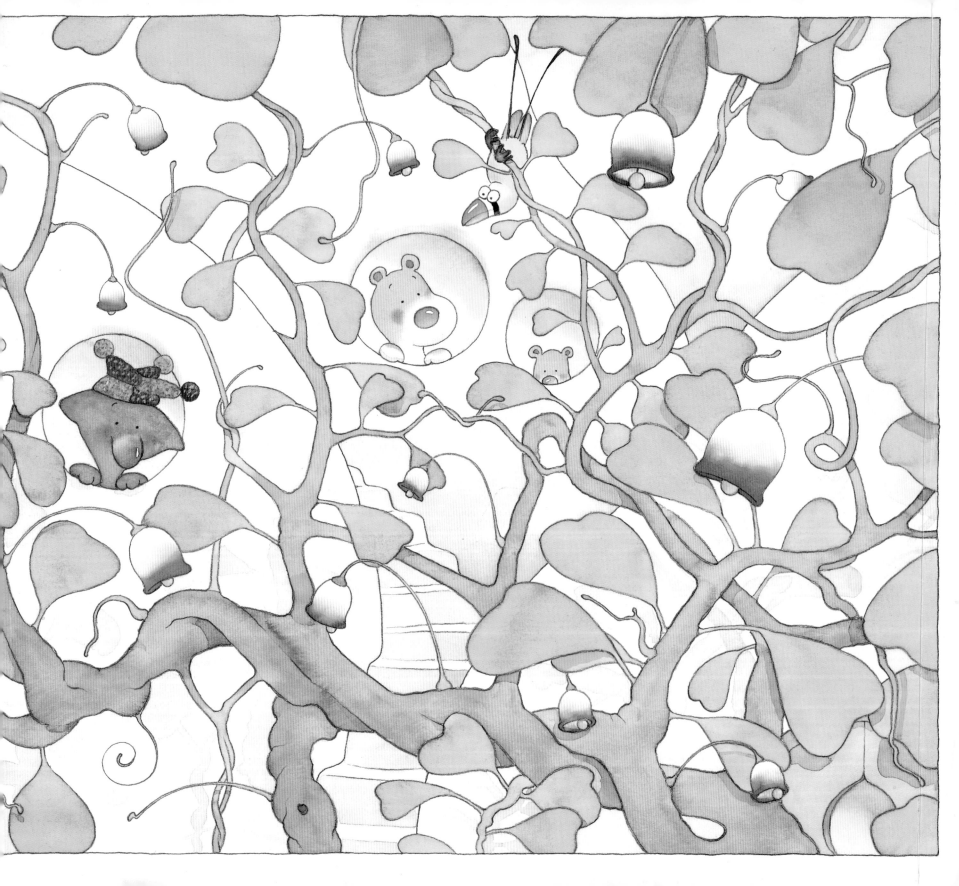

In Blue Nose Village
everyone has been kept
awake by Ploo's bellvine.
And, what is more, no one can
open their front door.
'We'll just have to chop it down!' says Ploo.
He borrows an axe from Hatz and climbs out of
the window. Dig follows. But the bellvine has
grown many branches and it is not long before
they are lost among the giant leaves. They scramble
this way and that, trying to find a way down.

At last something catches Ploo's eye,
something not quite green and not quite blue.
It is the corner of his own front door.

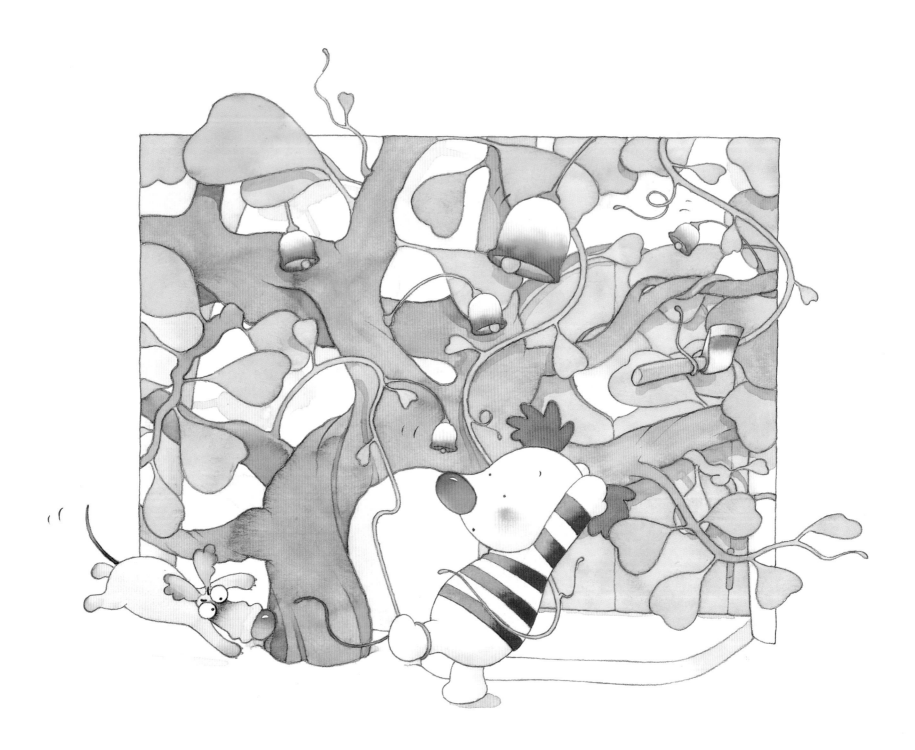

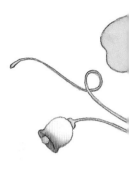

The trunk of the bellvine has grown thicker than Ploo himself, but he raises the axe above his head and swings. As he strikes, all the bells on the bellvine seem to ring at once. Clang! Ding! Bong! But the little axe makes hardly a scratch.

Ploo raises the axe again. But, before he can strike, something tugs it from his hand, and he feels a tendrily finger slowly wrap itself around his waist. Another curls around his foot.

Suddenly, there is Dig, barking and biting and scratching at the bellvine! The bellvine loosens its grip and Ploo kicks his way free. He squirms and wriggles as fast as he can, out into the blinding sun of Blue Nose Beach.

Dig, still barking at the bellvine, backs out from under the leaves and bumps his waggling bottom into a small, sandy mound. He turns around and sniffs.

A small, blue nose pops out of the sand. The beachmole. A few feet away, another nose pops up. And then another. And another. And more still, until the beach is covered in beachmoles! Dig is confused. He has never seen more than one. It is as if all the beachmoles on Blue Nose Island have gathered just for him.

He runs around in useless circles and jumps on Ploo!

Then, just as suddenly as they came, the beachmoles vanish, and a moment later a strange and wonderful thing begins to happen . . .

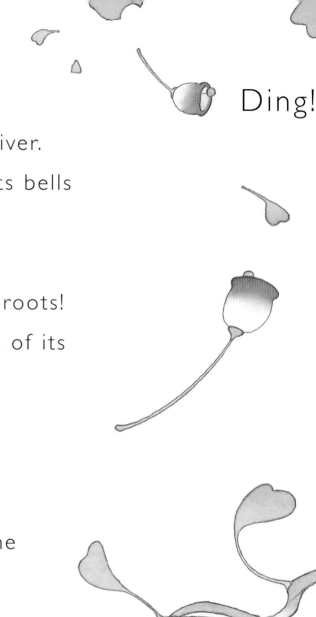

Ding!

The leaves of the bellvine begin to quiver.
Its tendrils begin to uncurl. One of its bells
falls to the ground with a loud clang!

What is happening, do you think?

The beachmoles are nibbling away its roots!

Its branches begin to shake, and more of its
leaves and bells shower down.

Ding! Dong! Clang! Bong!

Watch out, Ploo!

Ploo grabs Dig and curls up in the sand.
And with a great rending groan the bellvine
lets go of Blue Nose Village
and crashes to the ground!

Crrrumph!

When all the noise has died away, there is Ploo's front door waiting to let him in. He turns the knob and goes inside. And it feels so nice to be stepping over his own doorstep, that he goes in and out three times.

Then he shuts the door behind him, and waits for Dig to come and scratch to be let in, which he will do in his own good time when he has finished looking for beachmoles.

Everyone helps to clear up. There is so much of the bellvine that it takes all day to chop it up and pile it on the beach. By the time the last leaf has been cleared, the moon is rising behind Blue Nose Volcano.

'Let's make a bonfire!' says Hatz.

And that is the end of the bellvine, and very nearly the end of the story. But not quite.

As the darkness falls everyone gathers for the bonfire, everyone that is, except Ploo.

Ploo, you see, has discovered that the four remaining bellvine seeds have decided to grow after all, and he is off to plant them in the junglywood where they belong. Ploo has learned that where bellvine is concerned you'd better not wait till morning.

So off he trots into the night with the bellvines tinkling as he goes. And, as if in reply, the little honk owl honks gently from a bokonut tree. These are the only sounds, except for the hopeful snuffling of a small, blue-nosed dog following on behind.

Other books by Mick Inkpen:

The Kipper Books
The Wibbly Pig Books
One Bear at Bedtime
The Blue Balloon
Billy's Beetle
Threadbear
Penguin Small
Lullabyhullaballoo!
Nothing
The Great Pet Sale
Bear
Ploo and the Terrible Gnobbler